Community Helpers and Their Tools

A Chef's Tools

Holden Strauss

PowerKiDS press.

New York

Published in 2016 by The Rosen Publishing Group, Inc.
29 East 21st Street, New York, NY 10010

First Edition

Editor: Caitie McAneney
Book Design: Reann Nye

Photo Credits: Cover (background) Lebazele/E+/Getty Images; cover (chef) Andersen Ross/Blend Images/Getty Images; p. 5 CandyBox Images/Shutterstock.com; p. 6 Usawicka/Shutterstock.com; pp. 7 wavebreakmedia/Shutterstock.com; p. 8 tab62/Shutterstock.com; p. 9 Olga Miltsova/Shutterstock.com; p. 10 (measuring cup) M. Unal Ozmen/Shutterstock.com; pp. 10, 21 (measuring spoons) Ti Santi/Shutterstock.com; p. 11 Cultura/Zero Creatives/Riser/Getty Images; pp. 12, 21 (spoons) Richard Peterson/Shutterstock.com; p. 13 Diego Cervo/Shutterstock.com; p. 14 ifong/Shutterstock.com; p. 15 p.studio66/ Shutterstock.com; p. 17 StockstudioX/E+/Getty Images; p. 18 (tongs) keerati/Shutterstock.com; p. 18 (oven) Bacho/Shutterstock. com; p. 19 Monkey Business Images/Shutterstock.com; pp. 20, 21 (thermometer) Alexander Hoffmann/Shutterstock.com; pp. 20, 21 (timer) Jana Behr/Shutterstock.com; p. 21 (cutting board, peeler) Africa Studio/Shutterstock.com; p. 21 (stove) OZaiachin/ Shutterstock.com; p. 21 (vegetable brush) Janis Smits/Shutterstock.com; p. 21 (freezer) ppart/Shutterstock.com; p. 21 (electric mixer) trailexplorers/Shutterstock.com; p. 21 (knife) Shawn Hempel/Shutterstock.com; p. 21 (measuring cup) makuromi/Shutterstock.com; p. 21 (oven) photobank.ch/Shutterstock.com; p. 21 (refrigerator) toocanimages/Shutterstock.com; p. 21 (whisk) hawkeye978/ Shutterstock.com; p. 22 Jayme Thornton/The Image Bank/Getty Images.

Library of Congress Cataloging-in-Publication Data

Strauss, Holden, author.
 A chef's tools / Holden Strauss.
    pages cm. — (Community helpers and their tools)
 Includes index.
 ISBN 978-1-4994-0834-8 (pbk.)
 ISBN 978-1-4994-0835-5 (6 pack)
 ISBN 978-1-4994-0885-0 (library binding)
 1. Cooking—Juvenile literature. 2. Cooks—Juvenile literature. I. Title.
 TX652.5.S745 2016
 641.5—dc23
                          2014048747

Manufactured in the United States of America

CPSIA Compliance Information: Batch #WS15PK: For Further Information contact Rosen Publishing, New York, New York at 1-800-237-9932

Contents

Creative in the Kitchen

Have you ever seen the kitchen of a **restaurant**? Many cooks make the food you eat. The top cook in a restaurant is called a chef.

Chefs are in charge of everyone in the kitchen. They choose the **menu** for the restaurant. A chef has to be **creative** to make their menu the best in town. Chefs are community helpers because restaurants are important places where people in a community meet and eat. Chefs need many tools to do their job.

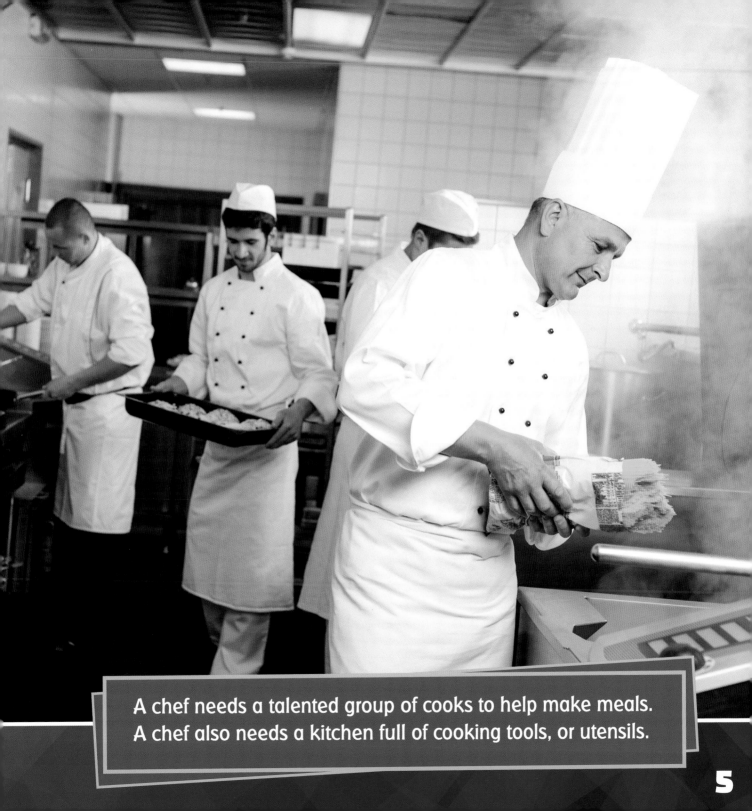

A chef needs a talented group of cooks to help make meals. A chef also needs a kitchen full of cooking tools, or utensils.

Preparing Ingredients

The first step in making a meal is preparing the **ingredients** for a **recipe**. Ingredients might need to be cut into smaller pieces. To cut food, such as peppers, a chef uses a cutting board and knives.

Chefs are **experts** at using knives safely. Some knives have straight edges and are used for chopping vegetables or cutting meat. Knives with sawlike teeth are sometimes used for cutting soft foods, such as bread.

knives and cutting board

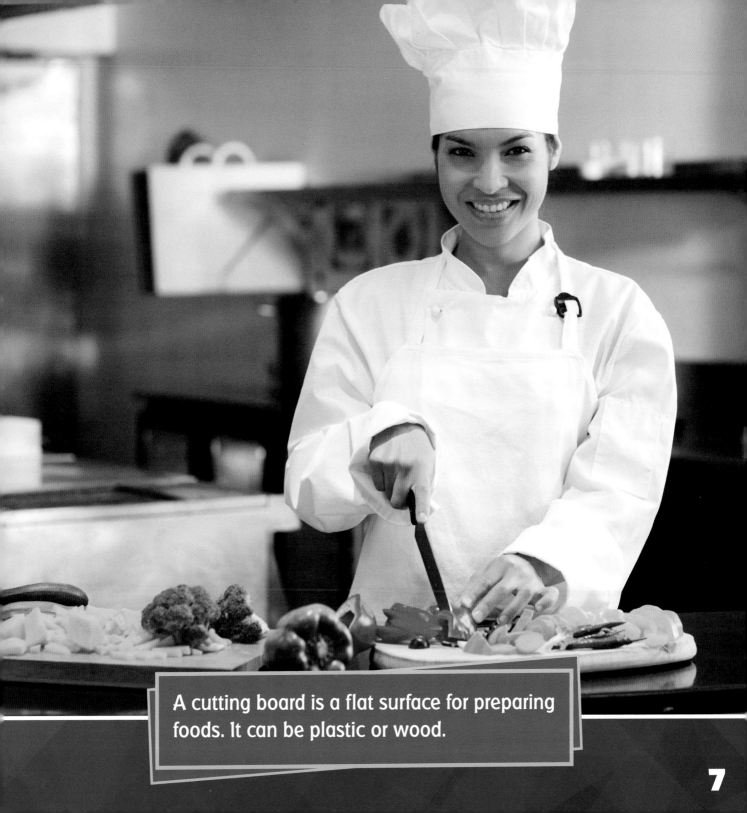

A cutting board is a flat surface for preparing foods. It can be plastic or wood.

Cleaning and Peeling

Some foods need to be cleaned and peeled before they can be chopped. Potatoes and carrots are good examples. Chefs use a vegetable brush to clean dirt from these vegetables.

A chef might use a small knife, called a paring knife, to peel the skin from fruits and vegetables. Another tool a chef can use is a peeler. Peelers usually have a dull blade with a **slot** in the middle. Chefs scrape the blade along the vegetable and the skin comes off through the hole.

TOOL TIME!

A paring knife has a short, sharp blade to "pare" foods. "Paring" means "cutting off the outside or ends of something."

This peeler helps a chef take the skin off a carrot.

Measure It Out

After a chef prepares the ingredients, it's time to measure them. Measuring ingredients correctly is the most important part of making a dish taste good! A chef measures ingredients like sugar, flour, and spices.

Measuring cups and measuring spoons are important chef's tools. A set usually has several sizes to choose from. A chef would use a measuring cup to measure one cup of vegetable oil. To measure smaller amounts, such as teaspoons, chefs use measuring spoons.

measuring spoons

TOOL TIME!

Chefs measure liquids in special measuring cups that have measurement markings on the side.

Measuring cups and spoons have numbers on them that tell a chef how much they hold. A measuring cup that holds one cup will say "1 cup" on it.

Stirring Ingredients

After a chef measures ingredients, they might mix some ingredients together. They can use a few different tools for stirring ingredients. A chef can use a spoon. Some spoons have slots in them, while others don't. Many spoons are metal or plastic.

However, many chefs use wooden spoons. Wooden spoons don't get hot when they're used to stir hot things. Wooden spoons are strong, so they can stir thick sauces and stews.

TOOL TIME!

Chefs often use wooden spoons for tasting hot foods cooking on a stove.

This chef is using a wooden spoon to stir and taste tomato sauce.

Mix It Up

Spoons are great tools for mixing, but sometimes a chef needs other tools. If a chef wants to mix ingredients until they're smooth, they might use a whisk. A whisk has a handle and a bunch of thin **loops** that help mix food together.

Some foods need an even bigger tool for mixing. A chef might use an electric mixer, which has two **beaters** that spin when the chef presses a button. The fast-spinning beaters can mix chunky foods until they're smooth!

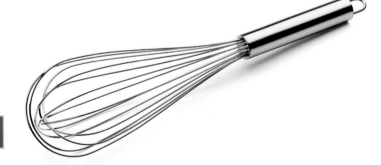

whisk

Have you ever used a mixer? This tool is great for mixing cake batter.

Keeping Cool

Some foods need to stay cold until they're ready to be served. This calls for a refrigerator! Refrigerators in restaurants are huge because they need to hold a lot of food. Milk, cheese, and meat are foods that need to stay in a refrigerator until they're ready to be cooked. Sometimes chefs put fruits and vegetables in refrigerators to keep them fresh.

Freezers keep food even colder. Freezers are good tools for keeping foods, such as ice cream, frozen until they're ready to be eaten.

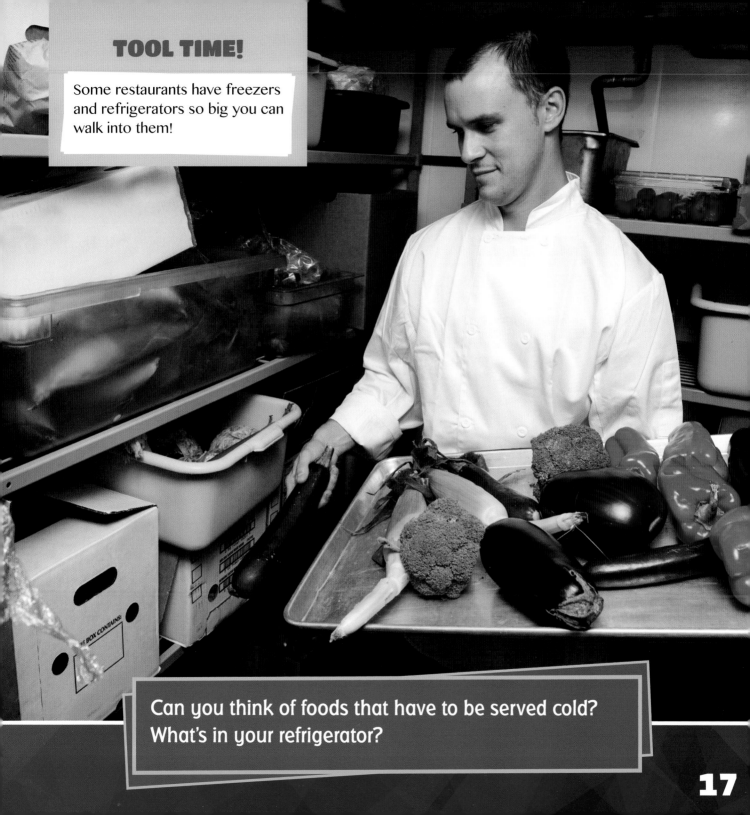

Some restaurants have freezers and refrigerators so big you can walk into them!

Can you think of foods that have to be served cold? What's in your refrigerator?

Bring the Heat!

Some foods need to be cooked before they're served. For that, chefs have very big tools called stoves and ovens. When you place food in an oven, it's heated from every side. Foods such as chicken or bread are usually baked in an oven.

Most ovens have stoves on top. Stoves usually have burners, which are circles that heat up. Some burners use heat from flames, while others use electric heat. Chefs set food on the burner in tools called pots and pans.

oven

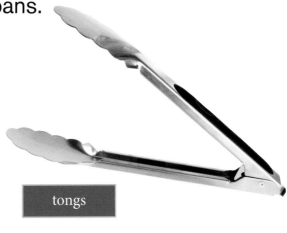

tongs

TOOL TIME!

Stoves can get very hot! Chefs have to be careful when they're using a stove so they don't get burned.

stove

This chef is cooking food in a pan on the stove. She uses a tool called tongs to move and flip the food so it cooks evenly.

19

Right on Time

An important part of following a recipe is cooking food for the right amount of time. Chefs need to be good at keeping time. They use a tool called a timer.

Imagine a chef is baking a cake for 30 minutes. If they cook it for less time, it might not be cooked all the way. If they cook it too long, it might burn! Chefs can also use **thermometers** to see if something is cooked all the way.

timer

thermometer

A Chef's Tools

preparing

cutting board

knife

peeler

vegetable brush

mixing

electric mixer

spoons

whisk

measuring

measuring spoons

measuring cup

time and temperature

timer

thermometer

cooking

oven

stove

cooling

refrigerator

freezer

Bringing the Community Together

One of a chef's most important tools is a recipe. Some recipes are found in books or online. Others have been passed down. The best chefs make their own recipes!

Chefs bring people in a community together to enjoy food and friendship. Chefs have many tools that help them make the best meals. See which chef's tools you can find in your own kitchen. Some are sharp or hot, so be safe. Maybe someday you can be a chef!

Glossary

beater: The part of an electric mixer that turns quickly to mix food.

creative: Having an ability to make new things or think of new ideas.

expert: Someone who has a special skill or knowledge.

ingredient: A food that is mixed with other foods to make a dish.

loop: A circular or oval object.

menu: The dishes served at a restaurant.

recipe: A list of ingredients and steps required to make a dish.

restaurant: A place where people can buy and eat meals.

slot: A thin opening.

thermometer: A tool that measures heat.

Index

C
cutting board, 6, 7, 21

E
electric mixer, 14, 15, 21

F
freezers, 16, 17, 21

I
ingredients, 6, 10, 12, 14

K
kitchen, 4, 5, 22
knives, 6, 8, 21

M
measuring cups, 10, 11, 21
measuring spoons, 10, 11, 21
menu, 4

O
ovens, 18, 21

P
peeler, 8, 9, 21

R
recipe, 6, 20, 22
refrigerators, 16, 17, 21
restaurant, 4, 16, 17

S
spoons, 10, 11, 12, 13, 14, 21
stoves, 12, 18, 19, 21

T
thermometers, 20, 21
timer, 20, 21

V
vegetable brush, 8, 21

W
whisk, 14, 21

Websites

Due to the changing nature of Internet links, PowerKids Press has developed an online list of websites related to the subject of this book. This site is updated regularly. Please use this link to access the list: www.powerkidslinks.com/cht/chef